the power *of* confidence

Also in the series:

THE POWER OF CALM

Sarah Jane Arnold

the power
of confidence

Unlock your inner strength

Michael O'Mara Books Limited

First published in Great Britain in 2025 by
Michael O'Mara Books Limited
9 Lion Yard
Tremadoc Road
London SW4 7NQ

EU representative:
Authorised Rep Compliance Ltd
Ground Floor
71 Baggot Street Lower
Dublin D02 P593, Ireland

Copyright © Michael O'Mara Books Limited 2025

All rights reserved. You may not copy, store, distribute, transmit, reproduce or otherwise make available this publication (or any part of it) in any form, or by any means (electronic, digital, optical, mechanical, photocopying, recording, machine readable, text/data mining or otherwise), without the prior written permission of the publisher. Any person who does any unauthorized act in relation to this publication may be liable to criminal prosecution and civil claims for damages.

A CIP catalogue record for this book is available from the British Library.

This product is made of material from well-managed, FSC®-certified forests and other controlled sources. The manufacturing processes conform to the environmental regulations of the country of origin.

For further information see
www.mombooks.com/about/sustainability-climate-focus
Report any safety issues to product.safety@mombooks.com and see
www.mombooks.com/contact/product-safety

UK editions:
ISBN: 978-1-78929-853-6 in hardback print format
ISBN: 978-1-78929-860-4 in ebook format

US edition:
ISBN: 978-1-78929-890-1 in hardback print format

1 2 3 4 5 6 7 8 9 10
Cover and design by Ana Bjezancevic, using illustrations from Shutterstock
Typeset by Barbara Ward
Printed and bound in China
www.mombooks.com

*This book is dedicated to my partner,
Mine – an inspiring human being; a kind
and courageous soul.*

contents

Introduction	9
Understanding our unwillingness	27
Beliefs and behaviours	43
Resistance	57
Increasing our willingness	65
Introducing mindfulness	81
Coping with failure	105
Helpful resources	124

'wheresoever you go, go with all your heart'

CONFUCIUS

introduction

UNDERSTANDING CONFIDENCE

Confidence. What does the word mean to you?

There's a lot of misleading information out there about what confidence is and how to build it. It can leave us feeling stuck, inadequate and confused. For clarity, we will first learn what confidence is *not* before clearly highlighting what confidence *is*.

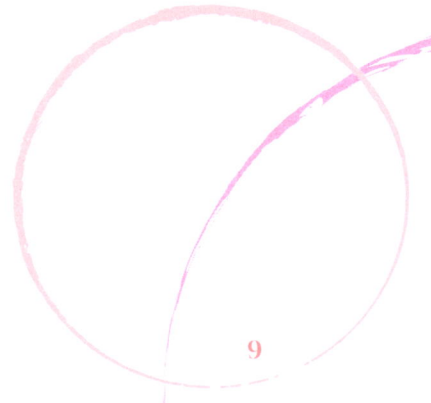

the power of confidence

Genuine confidence is *not*:

- **Narcissism:** it does not involve extreme self-interest or egotistical self-admiration.

- **Apparent competence:** when someone *seems* able to cope on the outside but struggles on the inside.

- **A pretence:** it cannot be built through the fake-it-till-you-make-it approach. In fact, pretending to do things with confidence implies it's *not* okay to feel unconfident or make mistakes, which contributes to shame.

introduction

Confidence is often context-dependent. We might feel confident at work but far less confident socially, for example. Confidence can fluctuate in accordance with other changeable factors too, such as stressful external events and our internal experiences (i.e. emotions, thoughts and how the body feels physically).

the power of confidence

Genuine confidence is unpretentious. It takes time to develop. When *all* three of the following aspects are present, a person possesses genuine confidence:

- **A self-assured feeling** with a sense of courage, competence and trust in yourself.

- **A self-reliant attitude** with an appreciation of our own abilities and qualities, and a belief that we can perform well and achieve a goal. There's a willingness to try, an openness to experience and constructive self-talk.

- **A positive action** – actually doing something new and challenging. There's the chance of failure, and the outcome may be uncertain but a confident person gives it a go anyway.

introduction

DEVELOPING CONFIDENCE

We're not born confident. Confidence is a skill that develops through social learning. We learn a lot about confidence via *modelling* (observing others). We watch how those around us conduct themselves in response to life's challenges — for example, their willingness to try new things. We develop ideas about what's safe and what isn't, who we are, who others are, what we can do and what we can't do.

the power of confidence

Our personality traits

Our personality influences how our confidence develops because it impacts how we behave. If someone is very shy, it's likely this personality trait will negatively impact their ability to build confidence – *if* no new social learning occurs. However, our personality need not predetermine our ability to build genuine confidence. How we perceive events, ourselves and others, and how we behave, **can change**. With guidance, emotional support, time and practice, we can learn new skills that can make it easier for us to build genuine confidence.

everyone can develop the skills needed to build genuine confidence

The process of building genuine confidence takes time. We're aiming to get to a point where we can experience the feeling of being confident, the attitude of being confident and the action associated with being confident in a particular context. To begin with, we need two key things:

- The *willingness to try* something unfamiliar.
- The *action* of confidence. That is, actually doing something unfamiliar and challenging.

introduction

The formula for building confidence then becomes quite standard:

1. Learn the skills you seek through one-to-one instruction or observation or study. Have a clear sense of *why* you're doing what you're doing – know your intention.

2. Try, keep trying, learn more, make mistakes, practise and apply your new skills.

3. Reflect upon the outcome when you try and alter your way of being accordingly.

4. Practise as much (or as little) as needed, until you can apply your new skills effectively.

the power of confidence

Remind yourself that it's okay to lack some skills, knowledge and experience right now. You *can* learn with time, good teaching, patience, compassion and encouragement. You may feel anxious and unconfident initially – and that's completely normal. If you've had little or no experience of doing a particular thing, then the chances are you won't *feel* confident doing it! What's essential is being willing to try.

introduction

NOTICING WHAT IS NEEDED

Genuine confidence is linked with our desires and values. It helps us pursue our ambitions, achieve our goals and experience a sense of fulfillment. It positively impacts our:

- interpersonal relationships
- work/career
- education
- leisure time
- physical and psychological health
- personal development
- role in community life

the power of confidence

Consider what you want to build confidence for. Reflection deepens our self-insight, clarifies what matters and builds motivation for change.

Imagine that overnight you've been given 'the gift of confidence'. When you wake up, what's different in how you think, feel or act that causes you to realize you're now more confident?

Positive change isn't easy. Even if we know what we need to do, the prospect of taking those first steps can feel daunting. It can feel like we need confidence in order to build confidence!

introduction

The Power of Confidence is here to help you. Specifically, to enable you to do two main things:

- Understand what gets in the way of you building and enjoying genuine confidence.
- Learn how to address these blocks, and overcome them, through self-help tools, like mindfulness.

the power of confidence

The techniques within this book are grounded in Acceptance and Commitment Therapy (ACT), Mindfulness, Dialectical Behaviour Therapy (DBT) and Cognitive Behavioural Therapy (CBT), all of which are proven to facilitate the development of genuine confidence. There are additional resources on pages 124–7.

With curiosity, openness and the willingness to read on, you can move closer towards a deeper understanding of your struggle with confidence. With time, patience, new learning, self-compassion and practice, you can become the person you want to be – the person you truly are.

With warm wishes,
Sarah J. Arnold

understanding *our* unwillingness

'be curious,
not judgmental'

WALT WHITMAN

understanding *our* unwillingness

What gets in the way of you building and enjoying genuine confidence?

We want to feel more confident in our abilities, so why do we often hesitate and avoid doing the things we want or need to do? It's not always due to a lack of desire. People commonly report that they really want to do X, Y or Z – but they 'just don't'. It doesn't make sense, does it? We really want to achieve something, but we don't do it.

the power of confidence

This can be defined as our *unwillingness to try*. The natural inclination to avoid challenging, uncertain situations, which could have 'unwanted' consequences, actually makes a lot of sense.

Simply put, these situations threaten us; they tend to evoke a stress reaction that can feel vulnerable and difficult to manage. They also highlight the areas in which we lack skills, knowledge and experience (which we don't tend to like much either).

IN THE BODY

When trying anything unfamiliar, we feel it physically. If we perceive a threat, our automatic flight/fight/freeze reaction is activated. For self-protection, the body channels its resources into fighting the threat, avoiding it or freezing in it.

The sympathetic nervous system generates our stress reaction and regulates the body's functions. Our glands release stress hormones that temporarily increase our heart rate, blood pressure and blood-sugar levels, and alter the digestion process – fuelling our bodies so we're ready to fight, take flight or freeze.

If the sympathetic nervous system is activated for a prolonged period (through chronic stress, for example), it will leave us feeling depleted. This kind of stress causes the body to respond in the following ways:

- Our muscles tense up, which can result in chronic aches and pains, tension headaches and so forth.

- Our breathing becomes more rapid, providing oxygen-rich blood to the body. This can cause panic, hyperventilation, pain or pressure on the chest, as well as feelings of dizziness and faintness.

understanding our unwillingness

- Our **cardiovascular system** enables our heart rate to increase in times of stress. This allows the body to receive the nutrients, oxygen and hormones needed to protect ourselves.

- Our **gastrointestinal system** affects how we digest food and absorb nutrients. Stress affects our stomach ('butterflies', nausea and/or pain) and bowels (diarrhoea and/or constipation).

It's normal to react in this way, but exhausting. If the body lacks energy due to confidence-related stress, it can stop us trying unfamiliar things.

EXPERIENCING CHALLENGING EMOTIONS

When we step outside our comfort zone and face something challenging, we experience an array of emotions that link with our stress reaction. For example, anger tends to be associated with our *fight* reaction; anxiety often comes with our *flight* reaction; and feeling overwhelmed, helpless and vulnerable tends to occur with our *freeze* reaction.

Our emotions have a significant impact upon our thoughts, body and behaviour. Many of us don't know how to deal well with our emotions, because we haven't been taught. Unfortunately, the more we judge our emotions, struggle with them and try to avoid them, the worse we will feel and the more it will impact upon our confidence.

it's our perception
of our emotions
that determines
their impact

FUSING WITH AUTOMATIC THOUGHTS

When we face the prospect of doing something unfamiliar that's challenging, the mind will think thoughts about it. Acting in accordance with our thoughts is an essential part of life. It enables us to problem-solve, develop relationships and live well. However, when our thoughts are influenced by stress, fear or emotional pain, they are less helpful. If we fuse with them, they can negatively affect our self-esteem. Here are some stress-related thinking styles, which can get activated when our confidence is challenged.

understanding our unwillingness

Black-and-white thinking: Seeing one extreme or another, and not recognizing the nuances. For example, judging an experience as a 'disaster' without seeing what went well.

Blaming: When things don't go as we'd hoped, we blame ourselves or others. We might blame ourselves for things that go wrong, even if we're not responsible.

Catastrophizing: Believing the worst outcome will definitely happen. This is the mind preparing us for an unwanted outcome.

the power of confidence

Comparing: Negatively comparing ourselves to others, especially via social media.

Empty positive thinking: Reassuring ourselves with phrases like 'It'll be fine,' which we don't really believe.

Filtering: Focusing on the unwanted aspects of a given situation – forgetting to consider the things that went well and what we're grateful for.

understanding our unwillingness

Mood-dependent retrieval: Having thoughts that match our current mood. For example, when you're feeling anxious because you failed at something and your mind recalls all of your past failures, too – along with other things that evoke your anxiety.

Over-generalizing: Making broad statements about how things are. For example, the mind says, 'I can't do *anything* right.' In reality – even if you make mistakes – you will do *some* things right.

Self-critical voice: Putting ourselves down. It's a thinking style that often comes up in times of failure and disappointment, when we're finding it hard to like ourselves.

the power of confidence

Shoulds: Regularly thinking 'I should've', 'they should've', 'you should've' is a consequence of social learning that creates inflexible standards about how things *should* be.

Worrying: Finding it hard to let go of anxious thoughts. Sometimes we focus on the obstacle ahead without considering what we can actually *do* to help ourselves and the issue. Worrying serves no useful purpose. It worsens anxiety and fuels self-doubt.

understanding our unwillingness

Take time to reflect upon how your automatic thoughts affect your ability to build confidence. If you're not sure, practise tuning in to them the next time there's a need for confidence and you notice that you're struggling. Approach your experience of thinking with gentle curiosity and get to know what happens in your mind, without judging it or shutting it down.

beliefs *and* behaviours

'human behaviour flows from three main soures: desire, emotion and knowledge'

PLATO

beliefs *and* behaviours

The beliefs and expectations that we hold, about ourselves, others and the world have a huge impact on our ability to build – and experience – genuine confidence because they directly influence what we do and what we don't do.

The following are some common expectations and beliefs that can inhibit our willingness to try, *if* we fuse with them (which we naturally tend to do):

'I have no motivation'

The mind may tell us we're *too tired*, we *can't be bothered* or we'll *do it later.* In actuality, there's *always* motivation of some kind. Either we feel willing to try and motivated to move towards a chosen goal, or we feel motivated not to. That sense of having no motivation is because our wish *not* to do something is greater than our wish *to* do it; trying might feel like too big a risk. Poor sleep, diet and lack of energy also affect our willingness.

beliefs and behaviours

'I'm not in the mood'

Intuitively, we prefer to wait until we feel prepared and motivated to move towards our goal before we take action. However, if trying evokes a stress reaction we don't feel equipped to deal with, most of us won't feel like acting. Resistance is a form of self-protection. Bear in mind that motivation increases during or after a task – as we gain self-belief, develop confidence through practice and learn that we can cope with our experiences.

'Anxiety is the enemy'

Many people believe that feeling anxiety is the problem. Common beliefs include things like:

- *Anxiety is a sign of weakness.*
- *Anxiety stops me from doing what I want to do.*

While these beliefs make intuitive sense, it's not anxiety itself that limits us; it's our *perception* and *reactions* to it. To cope, we judge our anxiety, attempt to avoid it, argue with it, suppress it, ignore it and distract ourselves from it. These control-based strategies tend to make anxiety worse.

beliefs and behaviours

'I'm not good enough'

As a result of past pain and experiences, many of us hold this belief. Comparing ourselves to others, we feel that we're not confident, smart or attractive enough. And fusing with this belief can truly limit us.

Faced with a new challenge, you may think: 'I can't do this.' You feel resistance. You believe that you're 'not good enough'. It's too risky to try, because you might fail, and then the mind will view this as confirmation that you're *really* not good enough. This greatly threatens a person's sense of self.

Not trying can create a self-fulfilling prophecy, and we deny ourselves the chance to succeed.

'I'm going to get found out'

Many people experience 'Imposter Syndrome' (self-doubt that arises from trying) when not-good-enough beliefs get activated. It's a burden that contributes to isolation, shame and fear.

Perfectionism is one way of coping with feeling not good enough – striving to maintain impossibly high standards, at all times, to feel adequate. It's not possible to live without making mistakes, so perfectionism only causes more suffering. It often leads to isolation. It fuels self-doubt and high expectations, and it inclines us to avoid new things – blocking our self-insight and ability to build confidence.

beliefs and behaviours

'Mistakes mean that I'm ...'

Reflect upon your relationship with failure. Here are some questions that might be helpful:

- Can you admit to making mistakes?
- What does making a mistake say about you?
- How did your parents deal with any failures?

Many of us *will* experience failure when we try new things. It's unavoidable. If we've come to view making mistakes as *bad* and *unacceptable*, and we believe they mean something fundamentally negative about us, then we will *not want* to step outside of our comfort zone and try new things.

'I'll do it later'

Procrastination is another way to cope with the possibility of failure. Deep down, we fear failure or disapproval and feel unconfident about our abilities; we might feel stressed, we may fear what will happen next, or we might prefer to focus on more pleasurable things.

Procrastination can only give temporary relief from discomfort. In the long run, it increases our stress and decreases our self-confidence. It can trigger self-criticism, evoke more challenging emotions (anxiety, guilt, panic and shame), and make it less likely that we'll achieve our goals.

beliefs and behaviours

'I need to feel in control at all times'

The wish to feel in control is part of human nature. However, some of the strategies we use to feel in control and find security and comfort are unhelpful. For example, perfectionism, procrastination and limiting food intake.

We get hooked into trying to control the things we can't control (our automatic reactions), and we lose sight of what we can control (how we respond to them). To manage the pressure that comes with trying to control everything all the time, many people engage in behaviours that allow them to, temporarily, completely relinquish control – like binge-drinking alcohol. This kind of coping behaviour typically brings more problems.

the power of confidence

'I'm not a confident person'

Many people tell themselves this, as if confidence is something innate that we either have or don't have. This can leave us feeling hopeless – if we believe our personality is fixed and there's nothing we can do to develop our confidence (which is not the case).

Consider how your beliefs affect your ability to build genuine confidence. Note down your reflections, and offer yourself some heartfelt praise for acknowledging these experiences. It takes strength, openness and courage. All qualities that will help you to build genuine confidence.

confidence is not a requirement to do anything, it is the by-product of doing the thing

resistance

'the greater the obstacle, the more glory in overcoming it'

MOLIÈRE

resistance

It's a block we're all familiar with. That strong sense of not wanting to do, feel or think something. The mind classifies certain experiences as threatening and uncomfortable, and for our own protection it encourages us to avoid them. For the same reason, we can also experience resistance to trying new things that we know would be good for us.

Another trigger for resistance is fear of success. Getting what we want can feel scary because then we'll have something that we really don't want to lose. The prospect of success can intimidate us just as much as the prospect of not succeeding.

the power of confidence

Reflect upon what happens when you feel unconfident. Notice how draining it can be to practise confidence as an action. Look at what we need to manage in order to do this.

There are also *benefits* to our unwillingness:

- We do things we already know we can do, and we feel competent and capable when doing these things.

- Life becomes relatively predictable and uncertainty is minimized.

- Our beliefs, expectations and core fears aren't activated so frequently, if at all, and therefore the raw accompanying emotions aren't felt as much either.

resistance

Unfortunately, along with benefits there are *costs* to our unwillingness: experiences we lose out on, such as ...

- Attaining a sense of competence and mastery of a skill or knowledge of a subject.

- Experiencing a sense of personal fulfillment.

- Developing self-sufficiency, personal freedom and new beliefs about ourselves.

- Building courage and self-efficacy (belief in our ability to accomplish a task and succeed).

- Building motivation for more positive change.

- Learning to trust in ourselves when we try, believing we can cope with the outcomes.

- Learning to trust in the process and accepting the outcome.

the power of confidence

- Holding realistic expectations; giving ourselves and others permission to make mistakes.

- Accepting and understanding our past failures, and learning from them.

- Experiencing a reduction in anxiety (when desensitization occurs).

- Experiencing a reduction in self-doubt (as skills develop and self-belief strengthens).

- Becoming flexible in our thoughts and actions.

- Building assertiveness skills.

- Enhancing awareness of boundaries, cultivating good judgement and gaining clarity on our values, sense of purpose and goals.

unwillingness has more costs than benefits – befriend your resistance and increase your willingness to try

increasing *our* willingness

'what you seek
is seeking you'

RUMI

increasing *our* willingness

Now we've gained insight into the key experiences that block us from building genuine confidence, we can focus on what we can do to help ourselves. If we can make the risks in trying feel less frightening – by imbuing ourselves with helpful skills, new knowledge and experiences – then we will feel willing to step outside our comfort zone.

Trying anything slightly unfamiliar and challenging will still feel daunting and probably evoke stress, but you can support yourself to feel more able and prepared to cope well with your experiences. This will help you to build genuine confidence.

THE CONCEPT OF VALUE-BASED LIVING

Many of us know what it's like to aim for arbitrary goals that we think we *should* achieve. Once we get that qualification, that job, that house etc., we move on to the next thing. These achievements can leave us feeling empty – without any real sense of personal fulfillment – *if* they're not underpinned by values that really matter to us. This is where focusing on our values is useful.

'Value-based living', also known as value-based action, is a transformative concept that comes from acceptance and commitment therapy. It's a way of being and living that helps us to:

increasing our willingness

- Know who we are.
- Come to like who we are.
- Act upon the things that really matter to us.
- Focus on the things that we can control.
- Develop genuine confidence.

Authentic, value-based living facilitates genuine self-worth and feelings of fulfillment. It positively impacts how we choose to spend our time, nurtures our self-esteem, encourages personal autonomy and develops self-efficacy – all of which help us to become more confident.

the power of confidence

Take a look at the following values and select some that matter most to you within the context of your life now. Then shine the spotlight of your attention on these values for the next seven days:

- Acceptance
- Adaptability
- Adventure
- Assertiveness
- Authenticity
- Bravery
- Charity
- Commitment
- Community
- Compassion

increasing our willingness

- Contribution
- Control
- Cooperation
- Creativity
- Curiosity
- Dependability
- Determination
- Discipline
- Empathy
- Encouragement
- Equality
- Fairness
- Fitness

the power of confidence

- Forgiveness
- Freedom
- Friendship
- Fun
- Generosity
- Gratitude
- Hard work
- Honesty
- Humility
- Humour
- Intimacy
- Justice
- Kindness

increasing our willingness

◆ Knowledge ◆

◆ Love ◆

◆ Loyalty ◆

◆ Meaningful work ◆

◆ Mindfulness ◆

◆ Open-mindedness ◆

◆ Order ◆

◆ Patience ◆

◆ Personal growth ◆

◆ Reciprocity ◆

◆ Reliability ◆

◆ Respect ◆

◆ Responsibility ◆

the power of confidence

- Rest and relaxation
- Romance
- Security
- Self-care
- Self-compassion
- Sensuality
- Stability
- Supportiveness
- Trust
- Wilpower
- Wisdom

increasing our willingness

Using this list as inspiration, write down your chosen values. Then set some specific, achievable goals that will enable you to live in line with each value. For example:

Values: self-acceptance and self-compassion

Goals:

- Try to notice and name my emotions when they arise.

- Practise accepting my internal experiences with compassion, as best I can.

- Do simple things for myself when I'm feeling emotionally challenged, such as making myself a cup of tea or having a warm bath, perhaps putting on some soothing music and burning aromatherapy oils.

the power of confidence

Values: curiosity and openness

Goals:

- Watch TED Talks and documentaries, about topics that interest me (aim for two this week).
- Try a guided mindfulness meditation and notice – with curiosity – what thoughts and feelings come up.

Value: connection

Goal:

- Message someone I care about this week and check in to see how they are. Let them know I'm thinking about them.

increasing our willingness

You may need time to reconnect with your values or establish what they are. Remember, your values are the principles you want to make your life about. These are not things you think you *should* care about; they are qualities you're genuinely interested in embracing. There's a commitment to doing this, in spite of the fear it may evoke. You're supporting your mind to understand that fear and resistance are *natural* and *normal* but need not stop you.

Focus your intention on what you *want* and *can do*, rather than focusing on what you don't want and can't do. For instance, aim to 'practise self-compassion', rather than to 'stop being self-critical'. Set yourself a conservative number of goals, and ensure they're realistic.

the power of confidence

You might notice some unwillingness when you're ready to begin your value-based living experience. This is completely normal. It's a new way of being that's unfamiliar. Remind yourself that you're choosing to open yourself up to all your experiences, both the pleasant and the more difficult ones, so you can live the life you want to live. There are skills and ways of being that you can learn (such as mindfulness) that will help you to do this.

greet your resistance warmly and thank your mind for protecting you from the unknown

introducing mindfulness

'be where you are;
otherwise, you will
miss your life'

BUDDHA

introducing mindfulness

Mindfulness is a skill that helps us to cope with our internal experiences, such as anxiety, insecurity, uncertainty and frustration. Mindfulness teaches us how to *receive* these experiences, how to *be* with them and how to *respond* to them in helpful ways. This reduces our suffering, encourages acceptance and increases our self-belief. It allows our values – more than our fears – to guide our behaviours.

Simply put, mindfulness is tuning in to the present moment, fully and intentionally, with an attitude of compassion, openness and curiosity. Overleaf is a simple exercise to begin with:

the power of confidence

Take a seat somewhere comfortable and quiet. As you engage with this exercise, regard your experiences with compassion, acceptance, openness and curiosity.

1. Close your eyes and tune in to the flow of your breath, in and out. Stay here with the breath for a few moments. Feel your feet on the floor or your hands in your lap for additional grounding if helpful.

2. Now, turn your attention to your mind. Describe your thoughts: 'I'm thinking about ...' You're simply noticing these thoughts; you're not trying to control them, judge them or push them away. Continue to breathe gently.

introducing mindfulness

3. Turn your attention to how your body feels. For example, maybe you notice a little tension in your neck and shoulders.

4. Notice your emotions and name them (as best you can); for example, curiosity, confusion, anxiety and hopefulness. See if you can allow them to be here with you, just as they are, for this moment.

5. Return to the breath and focus on breathing gently once more. Tune in to the sensations of breathing. Finish this exercise when you feel ready to.

the power of confidence

With mindfulness, we're conscious of what's arising in our internal world and making room for things to be, just as they are. We're not causing suffering by judging ourselves for our experiences, fighting against them or trying to run from them. If any of these stress reactions do occur, we greet them with understanding. We see them for what they are: a normal reaction to fear. We learn to greet our external experiences in much the same way by being non-judgemental, moment by moment.

The automatic experience of breathing is an anchor to focus our attention in the present moment. This practice might seem simple, but don't be fooled. The human mind can be like a wayward toddler – chattering about this and that.

introducing mindfulness

Keep in mind that you can practise mindfulness informally by engaging in any activity 'mindfully', such as eating or taking a shower. Simply tune in to what you can see, hear, touch, taste and smell. Mindfully notice your internal world too, while you do this. This is informal mindfulness.

Being aware that you feel unconfident sometimes is, in itself, a form of mindful awareness if you can acknowledge your experience with compassion. Along with bringing a greater sense of emotional balance, mindfulness enables us to achieve a greater sense of confidence in our ability to cope with life.

RESPONDING TO REACTIONS

Mindfulness is all about learning how to respond to our reactions when we're emotionally challenged. These reactions might come in the form of physical sensations, emotions, thoughts, urges and/or stress-related behaviours. The next time your confidence is challenged, see if you can mindfully notice the aspects of your internal world.

Mindfulness of the body

Try to hold a mindful attitude towards any bodily sensations you experience. Whenever you feel unconfident, use your mindfulness practice to notice where in your body you're feeling these sensations and describe them with a sentence in your head. Here's an example for you:

introducing mindfulness

'I'm noticing a fast, fluttery
feeling in my chest.'

1. Tell your mind these sensations are normal and will pass – it's your stress reaction trying to keep you safe.

2. Use your breath to support your mind and body if you need to calm down. Breathe in through your nose for the count of four – pause for a second – and breathe out through your mouth for the count of six.

3. Repeat this for a minute or so. It restores our natural equilibrium by rebalancing the levels of oxygen and CO_2 in the body.

Mindfulness of emotions

This essential practice supports us to understand our internal world, be *with* our emotions and respond to ourselves in a helpful way. Here are some core practices that can soothe you when you feel unconfident and emotionally triggered:

Naming emotions

Learning how to observe and describe our emotions helps us to acknowledge our emotional experience and identify our own needs. It can feel a bit tricky at first, but it gets easier with time, patience and practice. For instance, if you notice frustrated thoughts and tension in your body, say: 'There's frustration.' When you're on edge, think: 'I feel anxious.' Define each emotion with just one *feeling word*, such as, anger, sadness or anxiety.

introducing mindfulness

Accepting emotions

Knowing *why* we have emotions can help us accept and understand their existence. Our emotions, as raw and unpleasant as they can be, serve an important function. They're messengers that tell us important information about our experiences.

Emotions facilitate self-awareness, motivate us, prepare us for action, enable us to protect ourselves and communicate with others. They need to be evocative in order to get our attention!

Different emotions convey different things about our experiences, thoughts and needs, which is why it's so important to name our feelings. For instance, fear attempts to protect us from emotional pain, physical pain and danger. It warns us that our life, health or wellbeing could be under threat.

the power of confidence

When we're feeling unconfident and anxious, it's usually because one or more of these fundamental fears has been triggered:

- Fear of death.
- Fear of being physically hurt.
- Fear of being hurt emotionally (such as being disapproved of), which threatens our sense of self as worthy, lovable and capable.
- Fear of separation/rejection/abandonment.
- Fear of losing our autonomy/being entrapped and controlled.

Fear prompts us to protect ourselves: fighting against the threat, running from it or freezing. Our reactions are all attempts to escape danger.

introducing mindfulness

Acceptance of something doesn't mean you *like* it. You're simply acknowledging that your emotions exist, not fighting or avoiding them. This protects us from escalating our stress reaction. When we struggle with our emotions, we can feel emotions *about* our emotions, such as sadness about our anxiety.

Of course, accepting our emotions isn't easy – it goes against our natural instincts. Remind yourself that acceptance is hard. You're doing your best. Try to breathe with your emotions, creating space for them to just be. Learning how to replace struggling with acceptance takes time. It's a new skill to practise for your own wellbeing.

These moments of vulnerability, pain and stress can teach us a great deal about who we are, what our needs are and how we can ease our suffering.

Validating emotions

Validating our own emotions helps to soothe the mind, creating a sense of clarity and stability. Sometimes we understand our emotions; on other occasions we can't make sense of them, but there's always a reason – even if it's not yet clear to us.

Validation means reassuring yourself that what you're feeling is real and important. Remember that you are human and you're allowed to feel your feelings. They exist for good reason.

The acronym 'NAV' (Name, Accept and Validate feelings) can help you to remember these three skills. Remember to pause first, as soon as you notice your emotional reaction, and take one mindful breath. Then try to practise this technique.

Mindful non-judgement

Try to get out of the habit of judging your emotions as 'negative' or 'positive'. When we think of our emotions as 'bad' or 'negative', our stress reactions are escalated and our emotions feel stronger and louder.

Try now to think of all emotions as simply telling you different things. If it helps, refer to the more uncomfortable emotions as 'challenging' or 'difficult' instead. This acknowledges your experience without worsening your stress reaction, because difficulties and challenges can be managed and coped with.

Mindfulness of thoughts

When you're feeling unconfident and emotionally triggered, see if you can check in and identify what your mind is saying to you, about you and/or about the situation you're facing. Can you spot any stress-related thinking styles in your thoughts? Chances are, you may find some.

When you do, begin by naming them. For instance:

'I'm being a bit black-and-white.'
or
'Ah, there's my self-critical voice.'

This simple yet powerful technique helps us to *defuse* from the content of our thoughts; that is, notice we're thinking thoughts – that may or may not be helpful – and become aware of their impact upon us.

introducing mindfulness

After you've done this and *un-hooked* yourself from the story that your mind's telling you, it can feel a little easier to respond to yourself and your situation.

You might want to pause and reflect upon your thoughts more consciously in order to illuminate your needs, identify what's difficult and decide what you can do about it. Alternatively, you may wish to refocus your attention back on what you were doing when you noticed the thoughts, or *shift* your attention onto something else that's value-based if your current activity isn't. Try to retain a stance of compassion and non-judgement when you notice what your mind is doing or saying. It's just being a mind – thinking its thoughts.

More on managing stress-related thinking

Another way to defuse from your thoughts, when they don't feel constructive, is to describe the contents of your mind in more detail, for example:

'I want to accept this job, but I don't know if I can do it. What if I can't? What if I mess it all up and they fire me? I'll have uprooted my life for nothing …' In response, you might say:

> 'My mind is thinking quite a lot of anxious thoughts'; 'I'm experiencing self-doubt'; 'I'm having a thought that I might mess it all up – I'm feeling really scared.'

Try to add in some compassionate self-talk, too:

> 'That's completely understandable –
> I've not faced a situation like this before. It makes sense that I'm thinking about this because it's important to me.'

introducing mindfulness

Suppressing thoughts makes them more intrusive. Stay with the facts. Remember that you can have alternative what-if thoughts to bring about a different perspective, such as: 'What if I learn something? What if I enjoy myself?'

Mindfulness can be a great help when you're feeling unconfident and difficult thoughts pop into your head. When this happens and you're lost in your own thoughts, try to greet yourself with compassion and understanding.

Use the NAV technique (see page 92) to respond to your emotions and practise defusing from your thoughts. Then mindfully refocus your attention back out – on to what you can see, hear, touch, taste and smell. Repeat this process again and again if you need to.

the power of confidence

Mindfully notice your needs

Sometimes our thoughts can block us from doing the things we want/need to do. For example:

'I'm too tired – I'll do it tomorrow.'

When you notice these thoughts, establish the intention beneath them. For instance: 'I'm too tired – I'll do it tomorrow' may indicate that you feel hesitant about how to tackle the task. Or maybe you are tired and it would be best to rest.

Always check in with yourself and ask: 'Does this urge fit with my values right now?' If it feels helpful to fuse with the thought, then do so. If it doesn't, then reconnect with what matters in the moment (for example, perseverance).

Let your values be your guide. You are *choosing* how you want to act now, consciously and mindfully – for your own reasons – because *you can*.

introducing mindfulness

Mindfully notice your beliefs

It's not always easy to spot beliefs because they tend to be a little bit less conscious. However, with gentle reflection we can learn to recognize them.

Earlier in this book, we identified some common beliefs ('I'm not good enough', 'I'm a failure' etc.) that can negatively impact our confidence and willingness to try new things.

When you recognize these kinds of beliefs in your thoughts, see if you can 'un-hook' from their content and notice the voice that's speaking. Often, it's *fear* – sometimes it's *past pain*. For instance, you might say to yourself: 'That's the voice of fear... I'm scared that I'm not good enough.' This helps you to see that your past experiences and current fears are influencing your thinking.

the power of confidence

You're mindfully noticing what's going on for you, rather than judging it or battling against it. This can reduce suffering, facilitate healing and promote personal growth.

Acknowledge the idea that 'I'm useless' is the voice of past pain and fear, then take the time needed to process how this belief developed, mindfully acknowledge its presence and focus on gradually doing things that will build a new, more helpful belief, such as: 'I am capable of doing things well.' In time, the old belief will hold less power.

Value-based living can help you build new beliefs about yourself that will encourage you to thrive, such as *I am good enough. I am capable. I will make mistakes, and that's okay!*

it's easier to build
new beliefs than to
dismantle old ones

coping *with* failure

'the only real mistake is the one from which we learn nothing'

HENRY FORD

coping *with* failure

Sometimes, things don't work out as we'd hoped. Disappointment, heartbreak, anger and sadness are normal emotional reactions to failure, making mistakes and regret. Many of us aren't taught how to cope with these experiences, so we do our best with the resources we have. Blaming ourselves, blaming others and avoiding our feelings are some of the reactive strategies many of us use.

Here's an exercise to try. Take your time and write down your core regrets in life. For example:

- 'I regret not being more assertive with bullies.'
- 'I regret not doing the things I enjoy more.'

1. Close your eyes and breathe gently. Connect with what it feels like to recall these experiences. With every breath in, feel your ribcage expanding. You are creating space for any rawness and vulnerability … just for a moment. Place your hand on the part of your body where you feel this (perhaps your chest, tummy, head or throat) and gently acknowledge any emotional pain.

coping with failure

2. Welcome any resistance. Remember, your emotions are just messengers telling you about your experiences, thoughts and needs.

3. Take a long breath out through your mouth, and try to offer yourself the compassion and forgiveness that you might give a loved one.

4. Your mistakes need not define you. You can learn and grow from them.

Give yourself permission to be human and learn from these experiences. Are there themes in your regrets, such as being unassertive or avoidant? Remember, we're all a work in progress.

the power of confidence

Once you recognize a way of being no longer serves you, it opens up space to try a new way. Remember these points when mistakes happen:

- **Allow yourself to feel.** Express your feelings with compassion and non-judgement as best you can.

- **Adopt an open attitude to making mistakes.** Mindfulness can help you befriend the feelings, thoughts and stress-related urges to fight/flight/freeze that get triggered.

- **Adjust the expectations you hold.** You cannot get everything right, all of the time.

- **Be honest with yourself about your role and other external factors.** Stay with the facts; defuse from stories your mind may tell you.

coping with failure

- **Own your mistakes and forgive yourself with self-compassion.** Give yourself permission to fail, so you can learn from your experiences.

- **Live in line with your values.** Stand for what you believe in and practise being less judgemental towards yourself and others.

- **Reframe difficult experiences as a chance to gain self-insight.** Notice the qualities you can develop during challenging times, like courage, strength, compassion, kindness, forgiveness, solidarity and self-awareness. These all contribute to confidence.

- **Check in and see what you can do to help yourself or the situation.** Focus on what you can control and give yourself time to reflect upon this.

the power of confidence

Remember, people you compare yourself to will be comparing themselves to others, too. It's human nature. All of us are walking around with some version of the 'I'm not good enough' story; you're not alone.

Think of others as a source of inspiration. Admire their talents, aspire to develop the qualities you admire in them within yourself, but don't forget that you have many wonderful qualities, too. Practise noticing and appreciating all the things you can do well already.

PROBLEM-SOLVING

When we do unfamiliar things, obstacles will occur. Knowing how to make considered decisions when problems arise is an important life skill. With practice, it can dramatically reduce our sense of anxiety, help us to deal with specific worries effectively, increase our tolerance of uncertainty and build up our self-belief that we can cope even in difficult times. It can boost our confidence.

If we haven't been taught, or lack experience in using, these skills, then we won't feel confident (yet) in our ability to deal with uncertainty and practical problems. It's completely normal.

Here are some guidelines for dealing with problem situations that might be of help.

Notice

1. Clearly define the problem and identify its consequences. Stay with the facts.

2. If the problem feels large and complex, break down the problem into chunks and select the issue you want to focus on now.

3. Identify your end goal or aim.

4. Identify external factors (such as financial cost) and/or internal factors (such as emotions) that might make it harder for you to address this problem.

coping with failure

Plan

1. Write down lots of different things that you could do to address this problem and consider the costs and benefits of each option.

2. Select the approach you want to try (one that's achievable and feasible).

3. Break down your approach into smaller, realistic steps if needed, so you have a clear sense of what you need to do and when.

4. Reflect upon the external and/or internal factors you identified. What can you do to deal with them? Incorporate this into your plan.

the power of confidence

Act

1. Begin when you're ready and transform your plan into action.

2. Offer yourself some genuine praise for facing this issue and trying to address it.

3. Evaluate the outcome. Did your actions address the problem?

When tackling practical problems: notice + plan + act at your own pace. Give yourself the time you need to address what's difficult. Some problems are harder to solve and it's important to acknowledge this. For support, see page 124.

ASSERTIVENESS

Communication determines how we interact with others and how we relate to ourselves. Assertiveness can be defined as our ability to express what we think, feel and need in a way that acknowledges and respects our own rights – and the rights of others.

Social learning can have a negative impact on our ability to be assertive. We might have learned to communicate in passive, aggressive or passive-aggressive ways because that's what has worked before. We may feel reluctant to be assertive because we fear it might damage our relationships. We might not know how to be assertive.

the power of confidence

Assertiveness skills training tends to have a positive impact on people's confidence and sense of autonomy. It enables us to ask for what we need, express ourselves, develop a sense of our own self-worth and protect/defend our sense of self in a mindful way – without disrespecting others. The more we practise being assertive, the more willing we are to step outside our comfort zone and the more confident we will feel. Here are some key points to keep in mind:

- You are allowed to feel your feelings.
- You are allowed to express your opinions and beliefs respectfully.
- You have the right to be listened to.
- Your thoughts and feelings matter.

coping with failure

- You are allowed to change your mind.
- You are allowed to say, 'I don't understand.'
- You are allowed to make mistakes.
- You can choose to say, 'yes' and 'no'.
- You can set your own boundaries.
- You can choose to behave in a manner you respect and that respects the rights of others.
- You are allowed to walk away from situations and people that harm your wellbeing.

When we're being assertive, we embody these beliefs. We recognize that others have the same rights, and our treatment of them reflects this.

the power of confidence

Sometimes we don't know how to respond in a given moment, and that's okay. Pause, take a mindful breath and ask yourself these questions:

What do I really think about this?

How do I feel about this?

*Is there anything I need or want
to say in response to this?*

What do I want or need to do now?

Be as open, honest and empathetic as possible in your communications, and express yourself as clearly as possible. Use 'I ...' statements such as:

- *'I think ...'*
- *'I feel ...'*
- *'I would like ...'*

Listen to what is said back in reply. Avoid blaming statements, which can make others defensive and shut down the conversation. Be mindful of your tone, volume and body language while speaking. Avoid sarcasm, offer eye contact if possible and maintain open body language, which reflects willingness to communicate in a constructive way.

SUPPORTIVE INTERPERSONAL RELATIONSHIPS

Spend time with caring and receptive people who champion you and celebrate your achievements. Supportive interpersonal relationships help us to trust ourselves and build confidence; they positively impact our willingness to try new things and how we view and talk to ourselves.

Open your mind to different kinds of people who share an outlook. Friendly coffee shops, online sites (like www.meetup.com), sports and classes provide opportunities to meet others.

coping with failure

It's normal to feel anxious about meeting new people; it's outside of our comfort zone, but it can be a wonderful step, when you're willing to take it.

IN SUMMARY

Building genuine confidence takes time, courage, practice and lots of self-compassion, but it's possible. Once you understand your unwillingness, validate it, befriend your fears and learn how to cope well with the consequences of trying, then the act of trying becomes less scary. You never know, it might just become something that you actually want to do …

helpful resources

Acceptance and commitment therapy
Harris, R. *The Confidence Gap: From Fear to Freedom.* Little, Brown Book Group, 2019

www.actmindfully.com.au/upimages/10_Steps_For_Any_Dilemma.pdf

Harris, R. and Aisbett, B. *The Illustrated Happiness Trap: How to Stop Struggling and Start Living.* Robinson, 2014

Assertiveness support
www.cci.health.wa.gov.au/resources/looking-after-yourself/assertiveness

Robbins, M. *The Let Them Theory.* Hay House, 2024

Help with procrastination
www.cci.health.wa.gov.au/resources/looking-after-yourself/procrastination

Robbins, M. *The 5 Second Rule.* Post Hill Press, 2017

Books about mindfulness
Alidina, S. *Mindfulness for Dummies.* John Wiley & Sons Inc., 2020

helpful resources

Arnold, Dr S.J. *The Mindfulness Companion*. Michael O'Mara, 2016

Chödrön, P. *Fail, Fail Again, Fail Better: Wise Advice for Leaning into the Unknown*. Sounds True Inc., 2015

Chödrön, P. *Taking the Leap: Freeing Ourselves from Old Habits and Fears*. Shambhala Publications Inc, 2010

Kabat-Zinn, J. *Wherever You Go, There You Are: Mindfulness Meditation in Everyday Life*. Hyperion Books, 1994

Penman, D. and Williams, M.G. *Mindfulness: A Practical Guide to Finding Peace in a Frantic World*. Little Brown Book Group, 2011

Siegel, D. *Mindsight: Transform Your Brain with the New Science of Kindness*. Oneworld Publications, 2011

Williams, M. et al. *The Mindful Way through Depression: Freeing Yourself from Chronic Unhappiness*. The Guilford Press, 2007

Guided mindfulness meditations and more
www.franticworld.com/free-meditations-from-mindfulness

Segal, Z. et al. *Mindfulness-Based Cognitive Therapy for Depression*. The Guilford Press, 2012

www.themindfulnesssummit.com

www.tarabrach.com

Support for neurodivergent brains
Neff, M.A, *Self-Care for Autistic People: 100+ Ways to Recharge, De-stress, and Unmask!*. Adams Media, 2024

www.additudemag.com

www.drkenmcgill.com/2022/01/05/ten-steps-to-improve-your-emotional-self-awareness-using-the-emotions-and-feelings-wheel

Managing anxiety and panic
www.cci.health.wa.gov.au/Resources/Looking-After-Yourself

Powell, T.J. *The Mental Health Handbook: A Cognitive Behavioural Approach* (3rd Edition). Routledge, 2009

helpful resources

If you have gone through trauma (e.g., emotional abuse, physical abuse, bullying, sexual assault, etc.) and you know that it has negatively affected your confidence, I reccommend you speak to a supportive mental health professional about your experiences. You can find a therapist here:

www.bps.org.uk/public/find-psychologist

ABOUT THE AUTHOR

Sarah Jane Arnold is a Chartered Counselling Psychologist and author. She works for the NHS and in private practice, offering psychological therapy that is tailored to the individual. She supports her clients to understand their pain, break free from vicious limiting cycles, and respond adaptively to difficult thoughts and challenging feelings so they can live a full and meaningful life.

Sarah lives in West Sussex (UK) with her partner Mine, their dog Maya and Priscilla the bearded dragon.

You can find Sarah at:
www.themindfulpsychologist.co.uk
www.instagram.com/themindfulpsychologist